Capture The Dragons Treasure
By: Sean Williams

Copyright © 2021 by Sean Williams
Published by Sean Williams / Enlighten Servicing

All rights reserved by the author. No part of this publication may be Reproduced, stored in a retrieval system or transmitted in any form or by any means electronic, mechanical, photocopying, recording or otherwise, without the prior written permission of the author.

ISBN: 978-0-578-93487-7

The dragons treasure.

There exists a great dragon, and it guards a treasure that is beyond measure.

This is the map to its location, but I must first warn you of its ferocious nature.

Only the strongest of those who undertake it will succeed and return from this journey.

The journey we are already on, it was begun long ago, the dragon made us forget.

It took our memories to keep us from seeking its treasure, to keep us from knowing.

The dragon guards its treasure with great strength and yields only to the most worthy.

Those who are not worthy will get lost and be consumed on the journey.

So I ask you, will you venture out in pursuit of this treasure?

We face the dragon and claim the treasure or we are consumed by it without understanding.

Will you leave your comfort zone to face the unknown?

It is only fair to warn you that you will face death itself before success.

Only as you lose your life, do you find it, this treasure you seek.

If you are too afraid it is okay, the treasure is not for everyone, only those worthy of it.

If you seek to find the dragon's treasure, then continue reading.

If you do not seek to find the treasure…. Stop here… stay normal…stay ordinary. Stay.

For once you know, there is no going back, you can't unknow, and will be called forever more.

Some say ignorance is bliss, but that's not who I am.

I am here to help, but you must prove yourselves worthy, it is why you went out after all.

To the brave: let's get this show on the road. Turn the page.

Overcoming Death, on a journey in to understanding

Hello fam, I hope this message finds you. I have been searching for a way to reach you for a long time now, so that I can give you a hand. I cannot tell you what this book is, all I can say is that you will know what it is, when you know. I wish to tell you of a great treasure that awaits you in the human world that is guarded by a dragon.
I know what you might be thinking, "a dragon and a treasure? Yeah right, there is no such thing as dragons", but believe me when I tell you both those things are very real. Not all treasures are silver and gold. Some treasures are beyond human ways of understanding and expression. Before I begin my tale about the dragon and it's treasure, I need to ask you a question. The question I will ask you might seem a little vague at first and your answer might change as you progress through this message I have sent you, but I would like to ask you right now in the beginning of you reading it anyway.
This question I must ask, has been a touchy subject over the last few thousand years, but in order for you to understand who I am, and why I'm sending this message to you. I need to ask you to think about this question and all the highly contested sensitive concepts that it touches upon. Once you really think about it, channels will align inside of you and the truth of "who I am" will begin to make sense. This is something no one can simply tell you. In the deepest part of yourself, you already know. You might have just forgotten. It's okay. It is all a part of the plan. You lose awareness so that you can find it. You journey out so that you can come back. You will remember everything eventually, maybe even a bit sooner if I jog your memory. Ultimately you must make up your own mind though, on who I am, and when you do, you will know without a doubt who you truly are inside. I will not prove who I am or if what I'm saying is true. There will always be those who doubt. Their doubt prevents them from the treasure and their doubt is their own to overcome. Without further ado, the question.

The question is, "What do you believe?" It has been said in the past that "to believe or not to believe is the question" but many never really sit down, take some time and think about what it is that they really believe, in regards to "the meaning of life" as humans understand it. In regards to whether "God and Christ" are "real". In regards to will there be a "second coming" of "Christ" to the human world. In regards to whether there is actually a "heaven" and a place of eternal life and unending consciousness, where those who dwell there have all they need and are free of ignorance, suffering and desire. In regards to who they really are, what they are really supposed to be doing in the human world, and ultimately what is it all for? In regards to whether there is more to being human and living human lifetimes than meets the eye. This is a pretty big question, I know.

Many never really think about it because it can be really confusing. It takes quite a bit of mental focus and energy to sort it all out. It isn't easy, and can be downright uncomfortable. The level of thinking required to figure it out is far beyond normal human capability. This situation causes the meek to give up and turn back long before reaching the treasure. The meek find it far easier to just believe what everyone else believes without really thinking about it. They find it easier to just be told what to think instead of actually thinking. Easier to just do what everybody else does and ridicule anyone who is different. There are some things that cannot just be explained to someone. Like who they really are for example. Realizing that you are actually a child of God is just something someone needs to see for themselves. You can be told but until you see it for yourself you don't realize and know its truth. Not knowing its truth causes fear. Humans fear the unknown, they fear what they don't understand. The dragon preys upon that fear and uses it to control the meek and make them give up trying to understand. It makes them give up seeking the treasure and just settle down and become inert in its world.

I have asked you this question regarding what it is that you believe because I wish to help you focus your energy on your true self. The real you. You will need to be who you truly are if you are going to defeat the dragon and claim the treasure. When you are ready, you will know where the dragon is, and what the treasure is that he guards and you will be truly unafraid. I will not explain to you what I know, the way I know it, because you must reach down deep within yourself, into the source of all self knowledge to receive the answers to this question, to get a good grasp on them, and not have them just be fleeting. You must ask the questions inside yourself the way you understand them to pull the answers up out of the "inner wellspring" and receive them in a way that you can understand. Once you see for yourself, no one will need to explain it to you from then on. As no one can understand the answer to a question they have not asked. This is what is meant by "ask and you will receive". There are clues like this written through all scriptures, philosophies, art, t.v., movies and music guiding those who are strong enough to seek the treasure. The very fabric of human reality is malleable, holding its own clues to the treasures' whereabouts, that one wouldn't notice if they weren't aware of what they were seeing. The belief that human reality is not malleable is one of the ways that the dragon hides the treasure from the meek. The belief that there are no clues and there is no treasure, keeps you from seeing the clues that you have been given since the beginning. If you don't see them, you won't understand them as they are. This is one of the reasons that I asked the question "what do you believe" in the first place. You must choose what you believe. Sometimes believing is seeing.

This message has come to you because you have a great destiny. Now whether you embrace your destiny or not, that is a choice left up to you. I love a good hero story though, don't you? I even love it more when I realize I'm in one. My favorite though, is when I realize I'm not only in a great story, but I'm the hero of the story, on a journey, who finds his strength in time to defeat the dragon and save his family members. To find and become your inner hero is truly a great treasure.

Ever since the beginning of this generation, this knowledge that I'm trying to share with you has been given to others like you in the world. It cannot be given directly, but it has been given through metaphor and parable. It has been written into story after story in hopes that it would be understood. I'm going to do all I can to help you understand, but I will not force you to. You will still need to believe what you choose to believe. You either are, or you aren't. You must choose, "to be or not to be". This choice is what is known scripturally as "agency". It is this "agency" that the supposed "war in heaven" was about.

Much of the great knowledge that has come to the human world throughout all time has come in the form of stories. The reason for this is simple. It has been said that "no one can be told the truth, one must see it for themselves". Reminding the children of God of who they are, and helping them find the way home, is what Jesus was talking about when he said "build for yourselves treasures in heaven". This has been known throughout time as "converting believers". The reason prophets are killed. The treasures of heaven are its people, specifically its children. The children of heaven all are. Many who are lost in the dragon's world just don't truly know that they are. Save your friends from the dragon's entrapment and enslavement in its world. Do for them that which I have done for you, pass on to them this message. You must allow them their agency though. If they do not want to believe in themselves they don't have to.

I'm going to tell you a story of my own now, and after the conclusion of my story, I'm going to take the opportunity to point out a few examples of some of the great works of the past that included these clues to finding and capturing the dragon's treasure.

I will take a break from recording this message and get back to finish the message to you after I finish the story~ I call this story "Pretime"... As I mentioned before, what I wish to say to you might be easier to understand if I said it in the format of a story, so here goes....

Pretime

Our story begins with a king overlooking his subjects and being approached by his troubled queen.

I feel your concern for him. Come forward... I feel we must discuss some things, but be warned, do not ask it of me that I prevent him from going, unless you as well, seek to find yourself subject to the time out of our kingdom required to overcome selfish desire and end up accompanying him into the dark confusion and the insanity of the mortal world it contains. You know that we must all abide by the rules that protect the peace and stability of our kingdom, and the very reason that every one that comes into being must face the darkness and overcome it.

I know you are right. I apologize that I even considered such an idea. I only worry about his return, and hope that he returns to us soon, after hearing that very few return now, compared to when we... well, when I came. I fear that he will become trapped in the sleep and lost in the cycle of endless reincarnations, forced to become a never ending food and power source for the darkness...

Do not fear. He must go out. Surely you can feel the conflict building in him. Soon the will of desire that permeates even here will overwhelm him, he will be seen as selfish, and if that happens, he will need to be sent out as punishment for being overcome by selfish desire and disrupting the peace. It will be far better for him if he goes out on his own, of his own free will, at least that way he will be loved during his time out, and besides, most of his friends have already gone out, it will be hard to prevent him much longer. He needs to get stronger if he is to be the heir of our kingdom, and the journey is the only way for him to truly learn to stand on his own, and come into being who he truly is meant to be. He must see for his own self what happens when uncontrolled selfishness rules. He will need to remain out there on his own until he understands. It is what is best for both him and the kingdom.

I know, you are right, sorry again… can you tell me again about how it all began? I love the way you tell it, and it gives me hope when I hear the way you explain it…

Okay well, before you came to exist, before anyone else came to this state of existence, there was only I, only light. Nothingness and everything… so I spread out. I searched far and wide for something or someone other than me. But I didn't find anyone. So I sat down and wondered how long I would have to spend alone, and hoped to eventually find someone else like myself to share eternity with, and that was when I saw it… It was a tiny little thing, small as a shiny round ball and the color was black. I reached down to pick it up and it jumped into my hand. I opened my hand to look at it, and that was when it happened.
There was a loud C-R-A-C-K, and a B-A-N-G, and the little shiny black ball suddenly grew very large, very fast and enveloped me. It became incredibly heavy and I fell asleep under the weight of it. That was the first time I went to the mortal world.
I found myself in the dark world, I got to be amongst others there and I enjoyed it. I pursued and embraced my desire, I created children, knew the unconditional love I AM through experience, and saw the evil that lurks in and feeds upon the heart of humanity. I mastered myself, overcame my desire to remain asleep, revealed unto my children the

way, surrendered the world, and woke up. When I returned to this state, I found this… pointing toward the large light swirling with many colors and the infinity symbol connecting the light and dark dots. I found the darkness surrounding us.

It was not too long after that, that others began to come from the world, and you were among the first of those to come from the human world. It seemed that I had found exactly what I desired, company, here. I also knew that the children that I created in my sleep state and left behind in time out, kept that world in existence, gave it a power source, and made it possible for others who proved themselves worthy to be able to come here.

Then something changed, and many of the others who had come from the dark world began to act selfishly and decided to try and take over, and ended up getting sent back out to the mortal world. It was apparent that the will of desire and ego, while necessary as a part of an individual being's free will, functioning and identity, can be overwhelming to those who do not establish a solid foundation. This problem led to many returning to the world. So I also went back to sleep and returned to the mortal world to see what the problem was. I found that there were practices and teachings which prevented the full use of free will, that during the awakening process, others were assisting their exit and were preventing complete self mastery, self sufficiency and full surrender and so I scattered the knowledge of these practices to the depths of the darkness. I tried once again to reveal the truth to those children of mine in the mortal world, but realized also that they would understand only what they chose to understand, and had to leave them with the time they needed to choose to understand everything or not. Anything more than what I had already done meant forcing them to understand, which I will not. Again, I, of my own free will, surrendered the world and came home to the light.

When I returned, I noticed the darkness had gotten a bit closer, had grown a bit stronger, and knew that it was trying to overwhelm me. By engaging with it in an effort to change it, I was making it more powerful. I accepted that this meant that I could not return again to help them, as doing so would be giving more strength to desire and would increase the power of the dark and it's beast that rules it. I realized satisfaction in the balance between the light and the dark. I realized that for everything to continue, the balance is exactly as it needs to be, and for me to do more would ruin it. It is like a work of art created by a master craftsman. The craftsman themself decides when to stop working on it, that it is finished, and that it is perfect as it is, exactly as it needs to be, and doesn't do anything more to it.

There have been less returning from the darkness than there were when this first began, yes, I agree. It seems as though the consumed humans are trying to keep all those who come from the light, trapped in a sleep state, to enslave them and prevent them from understanding, just who and what they are, and thus are preventing them from achieving what they are there for and then returning home. Surely this is the dragons doing. It craves power. The dragon and its minions have found a way to trick the children of the light into endless reincarnations, to enslave them and I understand that this is what you fear will be his fate.

Although, those who have returned most recently seem as though they are worthy of being with us, and strong enough to exist here permanently and are stable in their forms and will not be returning to the dark. So I know that it is actually still possible for them to find inner peace. Self sufficiency and self awareness are not easy, they both require incredible strength and will power, but that is exactly what protects the peace of this kingdom. If one is to have unlimited power and strength, and the ability to do and create anything they wish, as all who dwell in our kingdom do, should they not first have self control?

The darkness of the mortal world gives those of the light the opportunity to shine. Everything is as it should be. Balance must be protected, or life as we know it cannot continue. If I go back to the mortal world again, to destroy the sickness and put a stop to their corrupted ways, all life energy will come back to me, yours included, and I will need to start all over again, back to the beginning. I would not like that, and might not survive suffering losing you. The darkness might even win and consume everything including myself and everything might just cease to be. After all, it was my desire for company that gave way to the darkness which got this all started in the beginning, and desire consumes if it is allowed to, and thus it is desire which must be mastered before they can return to this state, otherwise a permanent peace here is just not possible.

We must trust in him that he will find his way home to us, that he will make sense of the confusion and that the unconditional love that he is made of, will guide him to the hero he truly is, and back home to us again. The difficulty of what is ahead of him, though it is great, is necessary for him to become strong enough to exist amongst all who dwell in this kingdom with us, and necessary for peace to be maintained. Everything he needs to find, to do what he is going to do, to be what he is going to be, still exists there. It is hidden, and not known to be what it is, but he will find it and succeed, we must believe in him. He is from the light and will return to us once he is ready. How long it takes depends on him, and I will wait as long as it takes. I must.

Yes, you are right, I will wait as long as it takes also, and believe in him.

I will be taking him soon. You should go tell him that. Feel his response and then send him to me. I will speak with him on the way out, and tell him what I can…

Father, you called for me?

Yes, son. The moment you have been waiting for has come. Soon you will venture out into the dark and experience the world it contains. First, I would like to explain a few things to you before you go. It is my hope that on your journey, you will find the strength that I know you have inside of you, the strength to be the future leader of our kingdom, a keeper of the peace here.

Why father? Why don't you just be our leader forever?

Even I need to rest from the effort it requires to maintain life as we know it. If I go back to sleep without someone here who is strong enough and capable of maintaining the balance and peace of our kingdom, then all life energy will come back to me and everything and everyone we love will cease to exist. When you are ready, you will return, as the true heir to our kingdom, and I will rest peacefully knowing that you are strong enough to insure the continuation of our family and kingdom. I will be able to rest peacefully knowing that everyone is safe.

Why me father? Surely there are many in our kingdom who have the strength to protect us. Why not just choose one of them?

That is a good question. Look at that, pointing to the swirling energy with the infinity symbol that connects the light and dark. Now come to the edge and look down. Can you see all those down there in line to reenter the darkness?

Yes father, there are so many.

Well, those are all my children, all your brothers and sisters. They are in a spirit world, or a world between worlds, waiting to reincarnate into a new body in the dark world. You cannot see them all from here, but there are nearly 8 billion of them. I can feel them all. Some are incarnated in a sleep state right now in a world between worlds beyond the border, which you can't see, and some are between incarnations awaiting reincarnation, which you do see down there. Some of them are from our kingdom, created by those here, in the kingdom of light, and some of them are children that I and others using the energy that I left behind, created while in the dark world. All of their life energy comes from me, and it is my hope that eventually a great many of them will find their way home to this kingdom, but while out, they are sick, and must remain out in the dark world until they find the strength to overcome the sickness. The worthy heir of our kingdom will find the way to guide them home.

What do you mean, they are sick?

Well the easiest way to explain it, is to say that they have a sickness that is an inherent trait of the darkness. The sickness they are fighting to overcome is like a parasite that feeds upon their energy. It causes a condition of unconscious amnesia, in a way of speaking, they fall asleep, forget who they are and where they are from. Everyone who goes out into the dark, experiences this, for a reason. The veil of darkness removes all memories, all self awareness, and wipes the slate clean. This evening of the playing field happens so that one can prove themselves strong enough to overcome the sickness. It needs to be this way in order for them to prove who they truly are in their core, prove beyond doubt if they are meek or strong. It is for them to be able to prove if they are worthy of entrance into our kingdom.

Do you mean that I will also forget who I am?

Yes son, you will have to face the darkness and prove yourself as well. There is purpose in sending you, you see, all who come to permanently exist here in the light must have first proven strong enough to overcome the dark. The dark is a state of mind that is in itself pure desire. Pure selfishness is the will of the dragon that lives in the dark, and you must face it. It began in the very beginning when I first desired company, simply because I desired, and because of it, you and everyone else are able to exist, so I must allow it to continue to exist as well, and must allow the sick to remain there, in that world, unconscious of the truth.

I could easily obliterate the darkness in a moment, but then everything would cease to be, and I would have to start over, and be alone again. Everything exists because I will it to be so. Without the darkness continuing to exist, for example if I surrendered all desire for company all together, the kingdom of light that you call home and all your friends wouldn't be able to continue existing. By allowing it to exist and continuing to desire its and your existence which are connected, I allow the will of desire to corrupt any who are not strong enough, and without all of my children who come home, first overcoming the overwhelming nature of its influence, the peace of our kingdom cannot be maintained.

Maintaining life and the kingdom as we know it is a delicate balance. I must continue to desire company otherwise everything ceases to be, and desire itself drains one's energy which requires one to rest occasionally and regain strength. I have been maintaining everything for a really long time and feel a bit tired and could use a rest. The problem is, in order to be able to do that without everything and everyone ceasing to exist, I need to have a suitable replacement that is strong willed enough to keep everything going smoothly energy wise and leadership wise while I rest. It is my belief that you are that worthy replacement. I can see it in you. You must prove yourself worthy though, not only to me but to yourself and the rest of our kingdom. You need to get stronger in who you are, which is what your journey into the darkness is all about. Do that and you will be the solution to the problem that has existed since the very beginning. Once I am fully rested, I will once again awaken and take back over in order to give you a rest, and after that we can take turns, problem solved. So that is it, now you know everything there is to know in regards to what you must do and why. No pressure though...

As we are up here right now looking down on all your brothers and sisters without them being able to see us, there is an eternal controller of the dark world as well, it is the dragon I spoke of. The dragon came into existence as a byproduct of my desire, along with its world, and will exist as long as I continue to maintain the act of desiring company and thus maintain our kingdom. As long as the kingdom exists, so does the dragon, and as long as the dragon exists so does the kingdom. Everything is connected. The dragon holds the children of light who are not strong enough to overcome its sickness in the dark, and feeds off their energy to power its world and satisfy its insatiable desire. It lives eternally in its world as its leader, consuming their energy, without them knowing.

It exists in a state of being that is beyond their ability to comprehend as all those in line to enter the darkness cannot actually see us directly right now, no one down there or in the dark world has ever actually directly seen it. It inhabits many vessels in the leadership roles and the wealthy of the mortal world while rooted in the dark energy plane. The majority of the inhabitants of its world don't even believe that it even exists. Its powerful will of pure selfish desire keeps the sick distracted and consumed by the pursuit of unnecessary things to have and to do, to keep them busy and unfocused. You could say that the dragon and I have come to an agreement to allow each other to exist even though I don't agree with how it runs its world and the way it treats its people.

I accept that the agreement in turn allows both the kingdom of light and the dark world to continue existing which allows us here to be a family. This is the balance of life as we know it that must be protected. Let us finish this conversation on the way down, I will walk with you.

I hope I can do it.

I know you are strong enough to do what I am sending you to do. As I said, I can already see it in you, just believe in yourself. While you are out there, do what you must for yourself, and help all you can, but know that becoming self-sufficient, and to build your own strength of will, is the primary purpose of the journey out, and the reason that no one has been able to help the sick. Those who are there are all equal and must all find their own strength in themselves to help themselves. They must not depend on others to save them. The meek depend on others and must remain there because they choose not to do for themselves. It is selfishness that causes that, and selfishness destroys peace. They all have all the strength they need, they all have access to the components to make the cure they need, they just choose not to use it. Their reason is their own. They can do it if they choose to. They should not be forced to. They must be allowed their agency. The cure to the sickness already exists in the dark world, and it will forever, inside of them and outside of them, but it's identity has been hidden by the dragon and his minions, in order to trap the children in the dark. Just as the desire for company which maintains our kingdom and life as we know it exists in me here and outside of me in the dark world. As it is here, it is there. As long as he keeps them trapped there, he remains powerful. It is my hope that you can find a way to not only overcome the sickness but to also reveal the cure to be what it is, to all your brothers and sisters who are trapped there. There will be some that you just cannot help, or reach, some who refuse to believe what you tell them and that is okay. There is a good reason for that. Some must remain there, of their own free will, in order to protect the balance, but it would be great if you could help release some of the energy trapped in the cycle. Just be who you truly are. I know you will find the way to stir the hearts of our people. Show them the way home. Lead by example. Do what feels right. I know you can.

One more question, father.

If I am going to forget all of this, why tell me?

I have told you all this, because I didn't want to feel like I didn't tell you anything and just thrust you out into the dark confusion and the clutches of the dragon without at least trying to help you at all. Inevitably you will be on your own out there, but if you find and take the cure and begin to awaken while you are there, you might remember some of this, if not all of this. The cure has this shape, creating an image out of sparkling lights, of a long stem with a half circle top. It is not known to be what it truly is, and is called by a different name there. They call it manna.

We are here. Do you see the puddle?

Yes father.

Put your hand in.

The dark liquid vibrates and shimmers and begins to creep up his arm.

What's happening father?

The dark liquid covers his shoulder and then his face.

What is this father? Why do I feel like this? Am I dying?

I love you son.

The dark liquid pulls him in...

He travels through space, sees the earth, and a pair of green eyes beyond it. The eyes watch him, a falling star, as he falls. He gets closer and closer to the planet and as he prepares for impact, he sees a flash and lands in a soft dark red warm spot. Hearing a thump-thump, thump-thump, he falls asleep...

The messages completion

The dragon and its world is death and its treasure that you must claim is life, unending consciousness, not only your own, but your brothers and sisters as well, that it keeps the meek from claiming, the way to your own and your family members' passage into eternal life it has hidden. The truth of the life of the children of heaven. Those who prove unworthy of life venture into death, get lost and stay dead. They do not enter the kingdom of heaven, by their own agency. This small book is a message designed to show you the way. The way you must choose for yourselves.

So I asked you once before about what you believe. The reason I asked if you believe that God and Christ are real and if you believe that you are a child of God and if there will be a second coming of Christ into the human world, is simply, because I AM Christ. The second coming is happening right now, as you read this. It is okay if I tell you that I am and that it is, you will still need to make your choice on what it is that you believe.

I have come to awaken and unite the children of heaven and guide them home. To free them from their entrapment and enslavement in the world of death. To show you how to prepare the way for you to cure yourselves. How to master desire, and subdue it.

You can either choose to accept that I am what I say I am and hear what I'm telling you as truth, and do as I have recommended or reject what I have told you as a deception of a false prophet. Believe or don't believe. You still have your agency. You still need to make your own choice. The people in the time of Jesus had to make this same decision. Believe or doubt.

I am what I say I am, but I will not prove it in any way because if you doubt I am, then you require proof. If I gave the doubters "proof" then I would be removing their "agency". Even Jesus said that those who doubt him and require proof would have none, and there would be no sign.

It is said that when Christ returns that he would not be known by appearance, or any other sign, or proof, but by that which he says to you.

So I say to you, you are the children of the kingdom of heaven. The time has come for you to know you are. To know without doubt. I have come to reveal the hidden things to you, to give you the truth of the hidden manna, the bread of life of which you are to eat. I hold the keys to hades and death and I am reaching in to guide you out and back to life from whence you came. I will not force you though, you must choose to take the hand I have reached out to you or not.

If you believe, you are a child of God The Father, who loves you unconditionally, more than you can imagine. Believe you are a child of

God who loves you enough to send you a message to help you. Accept this message, seek a deep understanding. Not only of the words written, but what is being said. If you choose to follow the clues of this message I have delivered to you, then gather and do these things which I describe.

I have come to do battle with the antichrist, to show you what it has hidden from you. To expose its ways of confusing and misdirecting the children of God. To free the children of heaven from its deception. The truth I carry will set you free, if you accept it as such. To help prepare your way for ascension into the kingdom of heaven. To help you be ready. I know this sounds different and scary but I implore you to listen. Know that your father has had this plan for you since the beginning. It is the hidden purpose. It is time, you must prepare. Your father created the manna for this purpose, to help you prepare, the dragon's minions seek to keep you from it. They seek to make all of God's children meek and unprepared by taking away the awareness of what their father has provided them. I have come to show you what they have done in their attempt to lead you astray. I have come to help you know the way.

The hidden manna is psilocybe cubensis. The treasure of the field. To prepare the bread of life that you are to eat which will help you build your strength you will need a few easily attainable things. The bread of life is the cure to the sickness of selfishness, selfishness is death. If you seek to overcome, you need to put forth effort. You will need to gather and prepare the things on this list.

Brown rice
Vermiculite
Distilled water
Psilocybe cubensis spores (mushroom seeds)

½ pint wide mouth mason jars
Micropore (breathable) tape
A pressure cooker helps but is not absolutely necessary

Blend the brown rice until it is powdered. Or use brown rice flour. Combine with the vermiculite in even amounts 50%/50%. Mix thoroughly. Add an equal amount of water. If 2cups and 2 cups, then 2 cups water. Mix thoroughly. Fill the jars to the bottom of the threads. Make small holes in the lids. Wipe the lip of the jar clean. Fill to the top with dry vermiculite. Put the lid on, cover with tin foil. Pressure cook in boiling water at 15psi for 90 minutes. Without a pressure cooker, boil for 2hrs 30 minutes. Let cool overnight. The next day insert the spores inside of the sterilized jar on the inside of the glass using a syringe via the hole in the lid. Put a piece of breathable tape over the hole. Put the jars into a dark place that stays constant around 78-82 degrees fahrenheit. Wait a few weeks. Once the jars become completely white on the bottom with no gaps, or colors, the now white rice cakes can be removed from the jars and can be placed into a humid chamber for fruiting. The humidity needs to be at 90% for the psilocybe cubensis mushrooms to appear. Once they appear they will reach full maturity within 5-7 days. The mushrooms need to be harvested from the cakes and dried completely. A full dose of the cure is between 5-7 fully dried grams depending on bodyweight. Most people are not ready for what they will experience with the full dose. I recommend starting with smaller doses first like 1-3 dried grams and deciding whether you want to progress to the full dose. You could always just buy them from people who have mastered the process but I feel that that is counter productive. Depending on money to get what you need is for the meek. Some things you should really learn to do for yourself.

You can also learn to grow in bulk by using corn or grain, and once that is colonized adding the colonized grain to a sterilized bulk substrate made from coco coir/ vermiculite/ and gypsum. This method tends to be a bit more difficult than the brf cake method with higher contamination failure rates, because of extra steps, which is why I recommend all beginners start with the brf cake method.

I recommend growing your own manna as self sufficiency and the strength to be able to do for ourselves is part of what we are here to develop. Practice patience, practice fortitude, practice persistence. Believe in yourself, you can do anything you decide to do. Where there is the will in you there is a way for you. Build your strength. Learning to grow manna will help you achieve all these goals. If you wish to share with your friends go ahead, but inspire them to learn to do for themselves, for that is what it is to truly help them.

It is for this reason that I have not just given you the manna, but instead have shown you how to prepare it for yourselves, so that you can be prepared.

I AM the second coming of Christ, here to reveal the way, the truth, and the life.

From ALL I AM, ALL came forth, and to ALL I AM, ALL is attained. When you know your true self, you will understand all this and so much more. You are eagerly awaited in the kingdom of heaven. You will enter in, when you are ready, and not before. Be ready. Blessed be those who understand. Fear not, for you are the children of the kingdom of heaven.

For those who doubt, I AM who I AM regardless of your doubt. Your doubt does not make me doubt who I AM. Your fear and doubt will not change my course. For I have remembered ALL I AM, where I AM from, what I AM here for, where I AM going and will never again forget. Believe what you choose to believe. I'm happy for you, it was the choice of what you can believe in, and the choice to be meek or strong that was the very first gift I gave you. The choice to be or not to be. May you figure it out. I have come to save my children from the grip of death. To end their time out and welcome them back.

It is said that God created man in his own image, which is another way of saying God reflects upon himself, as in "time out" aka "the journey" being a period of "self reflection". So I would like to say this one final thing to you.

Whatever your belief is, that I AM, you are.

Best of luck in your pursuit of understanding yourself. See you when you are done.

~C~

Clues to the treasure through out time

So as I mentioned before, I would like to point out some of the clues hidden in the great works throughout time regarding the truth of this world, and the search for the dragon's treasure it contains. Once you begin to see the clues I'm pointing out, you will probably begin to see them in far more places than just the few references I share with you here. It shows up through various works as the treasure being sought. In scripture the treasure is frequently mentioned as "the pearl", which can be translated as "a pearl of wisdom" or knowing how to sort out what is truly important and of value from what is not. I actually encourage you to seek more examples in other places. There have been many "prophets" trying to share knowledge of truth through time, they do it in their own way, and their attempts are usually hidden in plain sight. One can look right at them and hear them and not understand them for what they are. They are all around, and yet many are unaware of them. This is what is referenced by the saying that Christ cured the blind and the sick, and helped them see. The simplicity of his way of explanation gave those who heard him awareness and understanding. The dragon and its minions kill the prophets (those who God speaks through and has charged with speaking on his behalf) who try to help the others, because the dragon and its minions are trying to keep the children of heaven enslaved in not understanding.

The Bible was one such great work, even though it is written in an old language that is difficult to translate and edited by men seeking to protect their incomes, which can lead to confusion which requires clarification by what are regarded as "scribes and Pharisees" (in modern times pastors and clergy). The business model of the business of "church" is to keep as many confused as they can, for as long as they can, to provide weekly guidance, and earn weekly collections. Like doctors who prefer to treat symptoms of sickness rather than provide cures for sickness, far better income long term if people stay sick. The Bible is still a great work though regarding the story of God and his children, being fashioned from dust or clay which "life was breathed into", and begins with the story of Adam and Eve, being tempted by a "serpent", (serpent is another word for dragon) becoming dissatisfied (selfish), and God's children being sent out, out of awareness of their father God, into a world of the serpent to do for themselves. This is one way of describing what is referred to as the "fall of man", and "the first death". It is also a way to describe when you began your journey. It is a way to describe your "seed of energy" breaking off from the whole of God as a blank slate, so that it can be placed in a body and go on the journey. It was your fathers plan for you to go out on this journey and fend for yourself so that you could become self-sufficient. To grow into yourself. To get experience. This is what happens on the journey to the dragon's treasure. You come into your own. There are many examples of this proving of one's self and facing trials throughout the Bible, Moses, Noah, the apostles but the most prominent one is Jesus. The concept of the opportunity of the proving of one's worthiness.

Let's begin with Jesus. Jesus Christ was an excellent example of a child of God who understood his Father's will, the truth of the dragon's world and the people of it and the purpose of the journey. You can see it in the things he said. He went about the world and the time he existed in, trying to help others understand. He faced death for doing it. For standing up against the dragon's minions and trying to help all of God's children. There were many recordings of the things he said. I will share some of them with you here. Ultimately Jesus was a profound "mystic", who upheld the practice of hiding mystic truths from the unenlightened by disguising the truths in parables. The malleability of reality poses significant risk to the mental wellbeing of the uninitiated. To be thankful for Jesus, is to be thankful for an opportunity to understand God as his children. To be thankful for God loving us so much that he would send someone to help his children understand. Not everyone understands the real living Jesus, and the depth of what he tried to explain to us, the inner meaning of his sayings. This book is my opportunity to help you try to understand, but you must put forth the effort to understand, and I am thankful for my opportunity and intend to use it to do what I came to do.

Let's begin with the clues from Jesus within the bible passages of the new testament, but I also recommend reading the Gospel of Thomas, 114 sayings spoken by the living Jesus, and will finish this section with a few entries from it. I will not translate the entire Bible for you. I recommend you yourself translating the inner meanings of what Jesus said. I will also tell you that the Bible is incomplete, unfinished, as the story of God's children is unfinished, still ongoing to this very day. Anyone can tell you that, after all, there were 12 apostles, yet only 4 apostles' accounts were accepted to be included in the Bible. The apostle Thomas's account of the teachings of Jesus were far easier to understand, but it was rejected at the time the new testament was assembled because the people who were high up in the ranks of the church (scribes and Pharisees who grew fat on offerings to the church) who decided what would be included in the Bible's New Testament didn't really want the people (children of heaven) to understand the teachings of Jesus. It is their business model to confuse people, make them misunderstand, and be the source of understanding. To keep people coming back and leaving offerings. This is why Jesus accused the churches of leading the children astray.

In the gospel of Matthew 5:2-12 Jesus talks about the blessed children of the kingdom of heaven and how they suffer through the journey through this world. He mentions that the meek will inherit the earth (which is a reference to them reincarnating due to failure to prove themselves worthy). He mentions the peacemakers being the sons of God (those who work to end the conflict that is not understanding). He mentions that you are blessed if you understand, and go about the world trying to help those who have been taught to believe that deceptions and misdirections are the truth, by sharing your understanding as he did, and are persecuted for your efforts, and all those who have done so in the past have been persecuted. To know that you are blessed when those who worship the God of this world, the dragon, and its worldly things, revile and persecute you and say all manner of vile things about you for professing your truth.

The saying that Jesus "walked on water" is a metaphor. It should be translated as "this world is a sea of insanity, a sea of selfishness, a sea filled with little "fish" (meek) who are not strong enough to control desire." It is this "sea" that Jesus walked above. It is like the idea of "superman" given by Friedrich Nietzsche. Someone strong-willed enough to swim in the sea but not get wet. Someone who could go through the world untainted. In other words, what will you do, will you shape the world or allow the world to shape you. Be sane or allow the world of insanity to make you insane. Be who you truly are, or be what the world makes you.

Matthew 5:13-16 references sharing your "light" or knowledge without fear. Finding a way to share, that helps others know that God loves them and is waiting for them.

Matthew 5:17-20 reveals Christ comes to fulfill the prophecy, that the worthy son, the heir to the kingdom of heaven will come to rescue the children of heaven from the dragon's enslavement in the world of death. That the scribes and the Pharisees were not righteous, but rather were selfish and were misleading the children of heaven for personal gain. He will lead the children of God back to the kingdom of heaven. (this is what caused the scribes and the Pharisees to plot against him, to have him crucified. They saw him as competition and the reason they got less "offerings")

Matthew 5:21-48 Deals with the way of being of a person that is a child of God. Understanding that God is "perfect" meaning fully self controlled, strong willed and decisive, honest and unconditionally loving, forgiving and accepting, always seeking the best decision even when it means less share or no share at all of the rewards of this world. One who has overcome the desire for self gain. For the children of the perfect father to be as much of an example of their father as possible. To strive for the perfection that is self control no matter what the chaos does all around you.

Matthew 6:1-18 Is in regard to loving God for God's sake. Not to be seen by others as someone who loves God. In other words, don't do things for appearances. Do what is right because it is right, even if no one sees. 16-18 touches upon fasting. Fasting is the way to build will power, inner strength and self control. It is not for monetary gain. It is not for others to see you as someone who fasts for some appearance of "Godliness". To work on full self control is the effort to build strength and overcome the body's insatiable desires, which are the root of all what are called the "seven deadly sins". You are on the journey for an opportunity to build strength of will, to overcome "the will of the flesh", gain wisdom and strength, and know what you should and should not do.

Matthew 6:19-21 speaks of the treasures of heaven being greater than treasures of the earth. Everything began because God wanted company, or what are known as friends. Love your friends. Friendship is the greatest gift, God gave you an opportunity to experience what he desired in the beginning that got all this started, what he loved about the world, and what he keeps it all going for so that he can continue to have. 6:21 "for where your treasure is, there your heart will be also".

Matthew 6:22-23 speaks of the third eye, the eye of the mind. The eye of perception. Allow the light that is the child of God you are to shine. Be the light you are. Guide.

Matthew 6:24 One cannot serve God and covet monetary wealth at the same time. As monetary wealth is a treasure of this world, if one focuses on gaining it they become distracted and lose their way. Do not become attached to or pursue the things of this world. Just be who you truly are, all that you need will come to you. Don't want more than you need. As Jesus said in the Gospel of Thomas, saying 42, "be passersby".

Matthew 6:25-34 regards worrying about necessities. God has already ensured that all necessities are met. Those on the journey have all they need. Everything is there for them to do for themselves. Desiring more than one needs is being overwhelmed by desire and causes unhappiness and suffering, and ultimately the destruction of peace, which is what the journey is all about. Blessed are the peacemakers. Thou shalt not "want". Practice not wanting. Know peace.

Matthew 7:1-6 Don't be judgmental of others. Be accepting, Be unconditionally loving, Be forgiving. You don't have the right to judge anyone other than yourself. "Judge not, that you be judged not". Do unto others as you would have done unto yourself. Treat others as you would like to be treated. The idea that you can teach anyone anything, is self righteousness. It is the idea that you know more than others. When in truth, all are equal. All had the truth written into their heart from the very beginning, some just forgot so they could choose to remember or ignore. Simple truths should not be given to the unworthy, for they will deny them, and ridicule you for being different. Do not judge them as unworthy. First believe in them that they can, and help them prove their worth, let them make their choice, give them the manna if they choose to have it. Then once they thirst for knowledge, then they can be given the pearls of wisdom you carry. To judge yourself is to be self aware. To know oneself.

Matthew 7:7-12 Revisits what I mentioned earlier along with the concept that no one can be given an answer to a question they have not asked. 7 "Ask, and it will be given to you; seek, and you will find; Knock and it will be opened to you" 12 Therefore, whatever you want men to do to you, do also to them, for this is the law and the prophets".

No one should have everything explained to them. In fact no one can have everything explained to them. Some things one just needs to see and understand for themselves if they choose to. The reason that I am explaining this way of understanding, is simply because I wish that I had access to someone who truly understood the hidden meanings of the scriptures and could have explained some things to me in a way that was easier to understand. Someone to assure me that I would figure it out. Someone to tell me to think about the inner meanings.

Matthew 7:13-14 Regards the "narrow gate". So this one is regarding the teachings of the organized religious leaders "the scribes and the Pharisees" which the many follow, are the way of "the wide gate" that leads to destruction. Jesus accused the scribes and Pharisees of leading the children astray. "For narrow is the gate and difficult is the way which leads to life, and few are there who find it" This regards the difference between someone who seeks to be taught what to think, taught the interpretation of the meaning of scriptures (the wide path to destruction) and the difficulty and reward of one learning, interpreting and understanding the meaning of the scriptures their own way.

Matthew 7:15-20 Is the warning to beware of false prophets, and how to know if someone is a real prophet or a false one, is by what they are doing things for, the reason they create something, if it is for worldly wealth reward (self gain), or for the heavenly reward of bringing the children of heaven back to heaven (the fathers gain). The scribes and the Pharisees were clearly in their positions to receive worldly comforts. Many pastors and televangelists are pretending to do "the lord's work" in the face of the public but assemble mountains of worldly monetary wealth, expensive possessions, and become wealthy elites out of the public eye. They pretend to help others and put on that appearance, but are truly only "showmen" trying to help build worldly treasures for themselves.

Matthew 7:21-23 This is probably my favorite. It refers to the false prophets who amass worldly fortunes from prophesying in God and Jesus's name, from pretending to cast out demons in people in God and Jesus's name for a holy appearance to gain followers who will then give them donations and who have claimed to have done many wonders in God and Jesus's name, but truly all in the pursuit of worldly wealth who at the end of their worldly lives get to the gates of the kingdom of heaven, the gate to life, but are rebuked, 23 "And I will declare to them, "I never knew you, depart from me (life) you who practice lawlessness". (lawlessness= gave in to uncontrolled selfish desire and deceptive ways, not strong) They are cast back as little fish.

Matthew 7:24-27 Jesus refers to those who can choose to hear the depth of what he is saying, understand the meaning of the sayings, and follow his guidance (hears the sayings and does them) will be likened to a wise man who built his house on the rock. (the strong stable ground) who can withstand the test of the journey no matter what the journey throws at him. But those who choose to ignore and not understand and not do are the foolish (unstable) meek who cannot withstand the test of the journey.

Matthew 8, 9,10 Are stories of Jesus's various "healings" of which the "scribes" proclaimed him a blasphemer, and Jesus telling his apostles to go help all others they can.

Matthew 11:10 "For this is he of whom it is written" "Behold, I send my messenger before Your face. Who will prepare Your way before You."

Matthew 11:25-30 reveals that No one knows the Son except the Father, nor does anyone know the Father except the Son, and the one to whom the Son wills to reveal him (decides to reveal himself to, to be who he is, the coming out). It also speaks of the difference between leadership styles of the enslavement of the human world the meek reincarnate into over and over again without true rest and the kingdom of heaven (life) one goes to once they prove themselves worthy of it. 29 Take my yoke upon you and learn from me, for I am gentle and lowly in heart, and you will find rest for your souls. 30 for my yoke (direction) is easy and my burden is light.

Matthew 12:38-39 talks about "the scribes and the Pharisees" (who doubted him) wanting a sign of proof from Jesus. Jesus responded "An evil and adulterous generation seeks after a sign, and no sign will be given except the sign of the prophet Jonah." (The story of Jonah is of a man who is selected by God to prophesy in a specific town, but denies and instead boards a ship to a different town which is then caught in a storm. Jonah is thrown overboard by the crew and swallowed by a fish. He spends three days in the belly of the fish until he finally agrees to do the will of God and is then vomited out by the fish upon the shore of the town God originally told him to go to.) In other words if you are chosen to do, chaos will ensue if you choose not to do, things will just get worse and worse until you finally agree to do what you are chosen to do. It is better to not fight your calling. Just do it.

Matthew 13:1-17 Jesus delivers a parable to people who had come to hear him speak. The parable was regarding a sower who was sowing seeds. Some of the seeds fell in various unsuitable places and did not root or were scorched by the sun or birds ate them, but some fell upon prepared ground (suitable places) and became fine plants who yielded well. 10 When the disciples asked him why he spoke to them in parables he replied, "Because it has been given to you to know the mysteries of the kingdom of heaven, but to them it has not been given". 13 "therefore I speak to them in parables, because seeing they do not see, and hearing they do not hear, nor do they understand. 14 and in them the prophecy of Isaiah is fulfilled, which says "hearing you will hear and shall not understand, and seeing you will see and not perceive; for the hearts of this people have grown dull. Their ears are hard of hearing, and their eyes have closed. Lest they should see with their eyes and hear with their ears, lest they should understand with their hearts and turn. So that I should heal them. 16 but blessed are your eyes for they see, and your ears for they hear; 17 for assuredly, I say to you that many prophets and righteous men desired to see what you see, and did not see it, and to hear what you hear and did not hear it. (turn from the outward journey) (enter in) (the manna was given to know)

Matthew 13:18-43 include more parables, and some minimal explanation of their meanings.

Matthew 13:44 The parable of the hidden treasure! "Again, the kingdom of Heaven is like a treasure hidden in a field, which a man found and hid, and for joy over it he goes and sells all that he has and buys that field". This is referring to the search for the dragon's treasure that is eternal life and the pearl of wisdom. You will give everything for it. If you seek everything, you better be willing to give everything. Give up that which is not important for that which is.

Matthew 13:45-46 The parable of the pearl of great price! "Again, the kingdom of Heaven is like a merchant seeking beautiful pearls. Who when he had found one pearl of great price, went and sold all that he had and bought it." The pearl of great price is the dragon's treasure. It is the pearl of wisdom, wisdom that comes at great price. Give it all you got, to receive it. For you to ascend to life, it requires everything, all your strength. Full surrender. Only as one loses their life do they find it.

Matthew 13:47-52 Is the parable of the dragnet which speaks of the children of God that are the treasures of heaven on their journeys through the dragon's world and those who are selected to pass on to the kingdom of heaven because they have achieved what they came to achieve (the strong large fine fish) and those who are left behind because they did not (the meek small fish). Prove themselves worthy.

Matthew 13:53-58 Jesus speaks about people who knew him as a human, a normal person who was a "carpenter's son" and refused to believe that God was speaking through him. When he tried to speak to them, they were offended at him and he said, "A prophet is not without honor except in his own country and his own house". 58 "Now he did not do many mighty works there because of their unbelief." One cannot help those who do not believe one can.

Matthew 14 contains the story of the beheading of John the Baptist, and the metaphors of feeding the masses (eat the word) and "walking on the sea" and healing the "sick".

Matthew 15:1-9 accuses the scribes and Pharisees of being hypocrites practicing useless traditions. He refers to a prophecy by Isaiah saying, "These people draw near to Me with their mouth, and honor Me with their lips, but their heart is far from Me, and in vain they worship Me, teaching as doctrines the commandments of men.

God knows what is in their hearts, and why they do and say the things they do and say. They do and say for worldly wealth, not for God.

Matthew 15:10-14 Jesus calls everyone who wants to hear what he has to say to listen, and says, "Hear and understand: Not what goes into the mouth defiles a man, but what comes out of the mouth defiles a man" (meaning eating anything is okay, but pretending to be of God or speak for God in pursuit of worldly wealth is not okay, defiling) his followers told him that the scribes and Pharisees were offended when they heard that saying because they knew he was talking about them and he responded by saying, "Every plant which my father has not planted, will be uprooted" (if they are not true, they will be undone) "Let them alone (leave them be). They are blind leaders of the blind, and if the blind lead the blind, both will fall into a ditch". (they do not understand in themselves, nor can they help others understand in themselves) (one way to say, if they are dumb enough to fall for the decieving ways of the scribes and Pharisees, who confuse in pursuit of money, then let them be deceived. They will either figure it out or they won't.)

Matthew 15:15-20 Peter asked him to explain the meaning of that parable to them, to which Jesus responded, "Are you also still without understanding? (referring to the difference between true understanding and someone unwilling to put forth effort needing things to be explained to them, the meek need to have things explained to them, the strong seek understanding within themselves and put forth the effort to, the worthy come to full understanding) 17-20 finishes with clarification that man speaks from the desire of his heart, food goes in, but words come out, selfish man uses words to deceive, manipulate and get. It speaks of the pursuit of satisfaction of worldly desire.

Matthew 15:21-39 are metaphors regarding the belief of the faithful healing them and "feeding" the masses (truth).

Matthew 16:1-12 The Pharisees and Sadducees came to test him and asked for a sign from Heaven. But he rebuked them calling them hypocrites and left them. He was travelling with his disciples who had forgotten to take "bread" and Jesus warned them "take heed and beware of the leaven of the Pharisees and Sadducees". His followers spoke amongst themselves and after a bit more conversation with Jesus, 12 Then they understood that He did not tell them to beware of the leaven of the bread, but of the doctrine of the Pharisees and the Sadducees.

Matthew 16:13-28 Peter realizes that Jesus is truly a Son of the living God. Jesus proclaims that only God could have revealed that to him, and Jesus will give him the "keys of the kingdom of heaven" (the manna). Jesus predicts his worldly death and Peter tries to persuade him not to go to where he will be captured by the dragon's minions. Jesus tells his disciples that if any of them desire to go to the kingdom of heaven and eternal life, for them to deny themselves (overcome worldly desire), be the child of God they truly are, and surrender the world. "For whoever desires to save his life, will lose it, but whoever loses his life for my sake will find it". (you will face death before success, and you must be willing to. One must be willing to lose their life, to find it, the treasure, you are)

Matthew 17 speaks of being with Jesus and not knowing and understanding him as who he was and being afraid, but Jesus told them to arise and not be afraid. That faith in God's love and providence moves the mountain of doubt and unbelief in oneself that causes sickness, but requires practice, focus, and following to maintain. The kings of the earth (the dragon and its minions) demand that people pay them taxes and people do so the kings of the earth don't get offended and kill them or imprison them. They are parasites on the people of this world.

Matthew 18:1-5 Is a parable that reveals that humans need to realize the truth, that they are the children of heaven on a journey through the dragon's world to prove their worth. To humble themselves.

Matthew 18:6-9 Jesus warns not to get others trapped in the pursuit of worldly desire. The pursuit of unnecessary things.

Matthew 18:10-14 The parable of the lost sheep, 10 love the children, 11 for the son of man has come to save that which was lost (the children of the kingdom of heaven). 12-14 refers to a sheep who has "gone out" on the journey and experienced how rough it is out there, gained the knowledge that comes from that experience, who once found is cherished more than the other sheep who had never gone out and got the experience. Going on the journey creates strength, allows us to grow, and we are better for it. Once lost, now found.

Matthew 18:15-35 are parables regarding being unconditionally loving and sharing and having others try to take advantage of that nature and use you. To forgive them and explain what you feel to them. To be patient and forgiving with them because you want to give them an example of patience and forgiveness, for them to model. Be the light. For others to follow.

Matthew 19: 1-30 are parables regarding to overcoming desire for worldly things, like sex, expensive possessions, and that it is impossible to enter the kingdom of heaven (life) while being attached to the things of the world of death. Surrender them, and you shall live.

Matthew 20:1-16 is a parable regarding being happy and satisfied with what you have, comparing your experience to others' experience and thinking that you have done more than others who receive equal reward gives way to jealousy which causes unhappiness.

Matthew 20:17-19 Jesus predicts his "worldly death" would occur at the hands of men who plotted against him.

Matthew 20:20-28 A woman comes to Jesus and asks for Jesus to take her two sons with him to his kingdom of heaven. He tells her that she does not know what she has asked for, (that she has asked for her two sons to die in this world and to be taken to heaven) if they are willing to die to serve the children of God, to prove their greatness, prove their worthiness of eternal life.

Matthew 20:29-34 A parable of the blind beginning to see, regarding a simple explanation that enables those who hear it to come from a position of not understanding, to understanding. Those who heard it, and came to understanding, chose to follow him because they loved the way he explained. They recognized the truth in their hearts in what he said.

Matthew 21:1-22 The story of Jesus's journey into Jerusalem, and to the temple where he kicked out the tables of the "money changers" (offering collectors, temple tax collectors) and those who sold doves. He accused them of capitalizing on and making profit on those who went to pray. He called them thieves for trying to profit, and earn money in the temple.

Matthew 21:23-27 The chief priests came to him and asked him where his authority to speak in the temple came from, and he knew they were trying to bait and trap him, to get him to say his authority comes from God, so they could accuse him of blaspheming, and so instead of falling for their trap, he asked them a question about the authority of

John the Baptist, to which they out of fear, claimed they did not know the answer. He replied, "Neither will I tell you by what authority I do these things". This is a parable regarding a simple truth, "if you choose not to know, choose not to believe, you cannot be told. When you are ready to know, to be truth full, to believe, you will."

Matthew 21:28-32 regards doing what you came to do, the journey from not believing to believing. From not worthy to worthy.

Matthew 21:33-46 A parable relating to the dragon being given an opportunity to produce worthy children of the kingdom of heaven, but instead enslaving them and starving them and preventing them from understanding, and hiding what their father gave them. Instead of providing for them, helping them, supporting them and surrendering them to their father, fully grown, he captured them to keep them for himself and consume them. "The wicked vinedressers" parable reveals the journey through the world is to "break us" as in "tame us" to "settle us down" and make us suitable to be in the kingdom of heaven. Instead they (dragon's minions) prevent learning and profit from the bad behaviours that they trap people in a habitual cycle of doing.

Matthew 22:1-14 The parable of the wedding feast.

Matthew 22:15-33 The Pharisees and the Sadducees come to Jesus and try to trap him by asking him about paying taxes and asking about the resurrection. He talked to them in parables saying Give Caesar what belongs to Caesar, and give God what belongs to God. He explains the resurrection regards the children of God in the world of the dead, being taken up out of death. He tells them, "God is not the God of the dead (the dragon) but of the living".

Matthew 22:34-46 The scribes come and question Jesus to try to get him to falter but he doesn't and instead asks them all, "whose son is The Christ? To which they responded "the son of David" to which Jesus responded "then why did David call him "Lord"? "If David calls him "Lord" how is he his son?" No one was able to answer him, and because no one was able to answer him, they did not dare to question him anymore.

Matthew 23:1-39 Jesus speaks many parables regarding many things including calling the Pharisees and the scribes hypocrites who burden the people but do not carry the burden, who feast and enjoy niceties of the world off the backs of the people they take from and tell to go without. They put on the outer appearance of "holiness" but inside are the most consumed by desire (ravenous wolves). He accuses them of killing the prophets to protect their incomes, and being doomed for it. They were unwilling. "Blessed be those who know, those who come in the name of the lord, not in the pursuit of worldly wealth"

Matthew 24:1-51 Jesus predicts the destruction of the money hoarding temples and churches of men, the signs of the end of time, the coming of the Son of man to reveal the truth, and that no one knows when it will happen except the Father who knows his son only. For if the dragon knew the son of God was coming he would have prevented him from entering his world, as the dragon knows what the Son of God is there for. 43 "But know this, that if the master of the house had known what hour the thief would come, he would have watched and not allowed his house to be broken into. (the child of God is on the journey to capture the dragon's treasure, to take back all of God's children, the treasures of heaven) That all serve a master, knowingly or not, one either speeds up the coming home of the children of heaven (serve God) or they work to prevent it knowingly or not (serve the dragon).

Matthew 25:1-13 is a parable regarding being prepared, consuming manna helps one get prepared.

Matthew 25:14-30 is a parable regarding the gift of God being knowledge, and the difference between sharing the knowledge by those who receive it, which reminds the children of Heaven that they are indeed the children of heaven and thus returns them to their father, and those who are too afraid to be who (the chosen children of God) they truly are out of fear of ridicule and being called crazy who instead hide the knowledge God gives them, and they keep it to themselves instead of doing something with it. Having an opportunity and doing nothing with it is what is known as "sloth".

Matthew 25:31-46 is a parable regarding the welcoming of the worthy into the kingdom of heaven that is life, and the rejection of the unworthy, to remain in the punishment of the world of the dead. Every moment of every day we have the opportunity to prove our worth, by being caring and compassionate toward others, being willing and able to help them, but so many are able but choose to only help themselves. The worthy put others before themselves, the unworthy do not.

Matthew 26:1-75 The plotting of the killing of Jesus by the scribes, Pharisees, Sadducees, and the elders and high priest. Jesus knew they plotted against him because of his growing popularity. He predicted to his disciples during the passover feast (the last supper) that he would be betrayed and put into the hands of those who plotted against him, jailed and then crucified. He predicted Peter would deny him to save his own life. He goes to pray, to speak to God in himself and basically says, I would like to stay to help more, but if it is time for me to come home, so be it, may your will be done. Let my worldly death make it so the sayings you spoke through me, last in this world evermore and continue to help all those who understand them. Judas Iscariot shows up with those whom the chief priests and elders sent to capture Jesus. They capture Jesus and take him to be accused of blaspheming. Peter follows them and is spotted as one of Jesus's disciples and denies that he is, as Jesus predicted he would..

Matthew 27:1-66 The chief priest and others who plotted against Jesus turned him over to Pontius Pilate the governor. Judas Iscariot hangs himself in shame of what he did. The governor listens to the charges the chief priest and elders raise against Jesus, and asks Jesus if he has any rebuttal. Jesus says nothing. The governor's wife told the governor to let Jesus go. The governor tried to let Jesus go free and brought out a murderer named Barabbas and asked the crowd who they would like to be set free. The high priest and elders who had many people with them chanted to crucify Jesus. The governor feared an uprising and set Barabbas free, and turned Jesus over to the high priest and the elders to be crucified. They beat Jesus and tortured him and stripped him and forced him to carry a cross. When Jesus arrived at the place they intended to crucify him, they nailed him to the cross and stood up the cross for all to see and stood guard to watch and torture him until his body died. In that moment, the child of God that he was truly was returned to the kingdom of Heaven (life). There are various signs of God's disappointment in man, that man would do this, a large crack formed in the temple, the ground shook, and the rocks split. They take Jesus's body and place it in a cave and put a large stone over the opening of the cave. Pilate sets a guard at the cave entrance at the high priest's request, claiming that Jesus was a "deceiver" who had predicted, "after three days I shall rise."

Matthew 28:1-10 Is a story of two women who went to the cave where Jesus's body was laid and kept guard over. The women saw an angel who had rolled the stone off of the opening of the cave and sat on it. The guards were afraid of the angel. The angel told the women that the body of Jesus was gone because he had risen, and to go see for themselves. The angel told the women that Jesus was going to Galilee and to go see him there, and to give word of the news to his disciples. As they went to give word of the news, they saw Jesus and he told them not to be afraid and for them to tell his disciples to go to Galilee and they would see him there.

Matthew 28:11-15 The guards that saw what had happened went to report to the chief priests all that had happened. The chief priests bribed the soldiers to say that they fell asleep during the night and someone stole the body while they slept. As to deny what Jesus said would happen, is what actually happened. To prevent people from knowing and believing Jesus over them. They came up with a cover up story.

Matthew 28:16-20 The eleven remaining disciples go to Galilee and see Jesus. Some praised him and worshipped him, some doubted what they were seeing, and Jesus told them one final saying, "All authority has been given to Me in heaven and on earth. Go therefore and make disciples of all the nations baptising them in the name of the Father, The Son, and of the Holy Spirit. Teach them to observe all the things I have commanded to you, and lo, I AM with you always, even to the end of the age.

The books of Mark, Luke and John share many similarities to the book of Matthew and the Gospel of Thomas. They all give an account of the life, teachings and sayings of Jesus. I encourage you to read them yourself and draw your own understanding of the inner meanings.

There is no understanding better than your own understanding that you come to once putting in the effort to understand.

There are a few gems that are unique to the respective books though. I will point them out but know that they require significant reflection to truly understand the depth of their meaning.

Mark 2:17 is a parable referring to "the righteous" being good to go, but the cure was for the sick. The cure is the manna, for the sick with worldly desire and attachment to death that the human world is.

Mark 8:35 "For whoever desires to save his life will lose it, but whoever loses his life for my sake and the gospels will save it" (the true hidden meaning and purpose of the Gospels, the journey separates the bold from the cowards, the strong from the meek, the worthy from the unworthy)

Mark 10:15 "Assuredly I say to you, whoever does not receive the Kingdom of God as a little child will by no means enter it"

Mark 12:38-40 Beware of the scribes (preachers) who harbor ill intent. (pretending to be sheep but inside are ravenous wolves)

Luke 15:11-32 The parable of the lost son. The son was given a share of the wealth of the Fathers Kingdom, an opportunity to do much, he then journeyed to a far country, and squandered what he was given on useless things, and grew tired. He began to want. He took up work farming and feeding livestock, but felt as though he was starving with not enough to survive with. The son comes to his senses, self reflects, and recognizes that he had squandered what he had been given and 19 "I am no longer worthy to be called your son. Make me like one of your hired servants" (he humbled himself and asked to serve the

Fathers will) The father came to the son and praised him and cherished him. 31 "And he said to him, "Son, you are always with me, and all that I have is yours" 32 "It was right that we should make merry and be glad, for your brother was dead and is alive again, and was lost and is found". (one gets lost in unworthiness and struggle until they realize they are unworthy, which can lead them to worthiness if they do what they need to in order to humble and reunite themself with their true purpose, understanding and helping others)

Luke 16:13-15 "No servant can serve two masters; for either he will hate the one and love the other, or else he will be loyal to the one and despise the other. You cannot serve God and Mammon". -Referring to one who serves God being here for God's children, and one who is sick with and only doing things for the desire for money and other things of this world which is serving (the dragon) mammon.- God knows what is in their heart- they may be able to lie to men, in pursuit of worldly things- but God will see right through them. ("depart from me, I never knew you")

Luke 17:20-37 are parables that reveal "the kingdom of heaven is within" that true understanding is from within, not told. The Son of man (Christ) who comes forth will be made to suffer many injustices and be rejected by this generation (because of the doctrines of the high priest, scribes, Pharisees, and Sadducees). That there are worthy and unworthy in this journey and in the end the worthy would leave the dragons world (the world of death) and the unworthy would not, because the unworthy are attached to their worldly things and life (Lot's wife "looked back", don't look back, let it go). Jesus felt that "the worthy" would understand his sayings and need no explanation, and that "the unworthy" would not understand.

Luke 18:1-43 are more parables regarding "the irritating get attention", "humble yourself", "Those who realize their true self, the children of God enter the kingdom of heaven", "those who have much worldly wealth, find it difficult to leave it, they are attached and cannot let go", and Jesus confirms the prophecy that (Christ) will be persecuted and killed by men in powerful worldly positions, but will rise to heaven afterwards. The blind man receives his sight meaning "understanding".

Luke 23:34 On the cross, Jesus said "Forgive them Father, for they know not what they do". Regards the difference between understanding and not understanding the truth of this world and what one's actions are truly doing. They were killing the one who was there to help them overcome death. He told them that they had no idea what they were doing.

Luke 24:45 Regards the risen Christ, "And he opened their understanding that they might comprehend the scriptures." (The son in the world of man, the dragon's world, who has united with his father). I AM that I AM.

John 3:16 "For God so loved the world that He gave His only begotten Son, that whoever believes in Him should not perish, but have everlasting life" (one can believe in Jesus and not truly understand him. Understanding the inner meaning of his sayings and following his directions are what is regarded by this saying, this concept shows up time and time again through the scriptures)

John 3:19 "And this is the condemnation, that the light (knowledge of truth) has come into the world, (through Jesus) and men loved darkness rather than light, because their deeds were evil" (selfish) (men killed Jesus to silence him because he was converting their "believers" which reduced their incomes. "evil")

John 6:22-40 are parables regarding "the bread of heaven being the hidden manna". Jesus ends up in Capernaum to people's surprise. The people asked how and when he got there, he replied, 26 "Most assuredly, I say to you, you seek Me not because you saw the signs, but because you ate of the loaves (of the bread of heaven) and were filled (with the light/ knowledge). 27 "Do not labor for the food which perishes, but for the food which endures to everlasting life, which the Son of Man will give you, because God the Father has set His seal on Him" 29 this is the work of God that you believe in him who he sent" The people asked him for a sign so they might believe in him. As their fathers who were led by Moses, were given the manna in the desert by God as a sign, as it is written, He gave them bread from heaven to eat" 32 Jesus speaks another parable to them regarding the manna "Most assuredly I say to you, that Moses did not give you the bread from heaven, but My Father gives you the true bread from heaven". 33 For the bread of God is He who comes down from heaven and gives life to the world. (bread of life, psilocybe cubensis mushrooms) 35-40 are parables in which the holy essence of life (holy spirit) one is filled with awakens after eating the manna, speaks through Jesus regarding finding and consuming the bread of life in order to overcome desires such as hunger, and thirst, for knowledge. Seeing it, but not recognizing it to be what it is, and believing it can help. That the manna is from God to help his children be prepared for the end and ascendance to the kingdom of heaven. To be taken up out of death to eternal life.

John 6:41-59 The spirit given to Jesus continued to reveal itself through parables and its purpose through Jesus. Those who knew him before his infilling of spirit, and those who were aware of his "worldly mother Mary and father Joseph" became offended at the claim that "he came down from heaven" but didn't understand that it was the awakened holy spirit given to Jesus after consuming the manna ("teonanacatl" God's flesh mushrooms) that was actually speaking through Jesus, the essence of the mushroom that said, 47 "most assuredly I say to you, he who believes in me has everlasting life." 48 "I am the bread of life" 49 " Your fathers ate the manna in the wilderness (pasture) and died" (did not continue to eat the manna in Canaan, instead went back to their old ways) 50 "This is the bread which comes down from heaven that one may eat and not die". 51 "I am the living bread which came down from heaven. If anyone eats of this bread, he will live forever; and the bread that I shall give is my flesh, which I shall give for the life of the world". Those who heard what Jesus said became offended because they didn't understand that God was speaking through him after he consumed the "God's flesh" mushrooms, about eating the manna mushrooms and proving their worth (the worthy let go). God's children eat the manna and die to themselves (ego death) in this world, but are then raised up to eternal life they prove themselves worthy of, for being willing to die and completely surrendering the ill will. (only as one loses their life, do they find it)

In Revelation, God was speaking through Jesus in a spiritual language.

Revelation 1:8 "I AM the Alpha and Omega, the Beginning and the End, Who is and was and who is to come, the Almighty"

Revelation 1:10 revealed by the apostle John, "I was in the spirit on the lord's day, and I heard behind me, a loud voice, as of a trumpet" 11 it said "write in a book that which you see as truth and send it to the seven churches which are in Asia"

Revelation 1:18 "I am He who lives, was dead, and behold, I am alive forevermore, Amen. And I have the keys of Hades and of Death" (regarding being sent into death on the journey through the Dragon's world, but overcoming it by using the Manna God gave his children and finding life eternal)

Revelation 2&3 are the letters that were instructed to be sent to the seven churches throughout Asia. They are also parable sayings meant to be interpreted. Here are some highlights.

Revelation 2:17 "He who has an ear let him hear what the spirit says to the churches. To him who overcomes, I will give some of the hidden manna to eat." (regarding psilocybe cubensis)

Revelation 16:15 "Behold, I am coming as a thief, Blessed is he who watches and keeps his garments, lest he walk naked and they see his shame" (regarding the one from God who comes into the dragon's world of death to steal back the children of God for their father)

Revelation 22:12,13, &16 "And behold, I AM coming quickly, and My reward is with Me, to give to everyone according to his work." 13 "I AM the Alpha and the Omega, the Beginning and the End, The First and the Last." 16 "I Jesus have sent my angel to testify to you these things in the churches, I AM the Root, and the offspring of David the Bright, and Morning Star."

In the book of Exodus is the first reference of "Manna" being given by God as good things provided as sustenance. The story of Moses is one of someone sent by God to free his children who were enslaved in man's civilization. The pharaoh, or Pharisees. It was a story designed to guide people to what manna is, though because the scriptures as a whole and Jesus's sayings are all meant to be interpreted by those willing to put forth the effort to try to interpret them, what manna actually was wasn't disclosed. There were clues though regarding its characteristics.

These are those clues: Early in the morning, as the sun begins to light the sky, just as the dew begins to evaporate, behold upon the face of the wilderness, there lay a small round thing as small as the hoarfrost on the ground. The coloring of which was like coriander seed and bdellium. God revealed to Moses that it was given to them to prove whether they walked in God's law or not. Bread from heaven, regarding bluish bruising where cut or touched. To prove whether they were worthy or not. Whether they would let go or not. The mentioning of hoarfrost is another clue pointing out mycelial fibers present upon the ground near the manna (mushrooms). All of these clues point those, who truly believe there is truth to be found in interpreting the scriptures, that manna was something real, guiding them to realize that psilocybe cubensis mushrooms are the "hidden manna".

Me telling you this, does not take away your agency, you can still choose to believe it or not believe it. You can still choose to do it, or not do it. You can still choose to let go, or not let go. You still have your free will. I have told you how, the rest is up to you.

I will wrap up this section with a few selections from the Gospel of Thomas, but ultimately, I only hope to inspire you to search all of these scriptures for your own understanding, for that truly is what Jesus was doing in this world, trying to help us understand. Trying to help us know. Those who seek it, will find it, if they keep progressing, don't give up and endure to the end. Do you want to know if it is all real? Well, follow the breadcrumbs of the bread of life. Be filled with the spirit and you will know.

Gospel of Thomas, a recording of 114 sayings spoken by the living Jesus.

Gospel of Thomas saying #1 "Whoever discovers the interpretation of these sayings will not taste death".

Saying #4 "The person old in days, will not hesitate to ask a little child seven days old about the place of life, and that person will live" a coded message (parable) regarding eating psilocybin mushrooms that grow to full maturity in seven days to overcome attachment to death and be prepared to let go.

Saying #35 "One can't enter a strong person's house and take it by force without tying his hands. Then one can loot his house." This is regarding the sons of God coming into the dragon's world to take back the children of God whom the dragon has entrapped and enslaved. The treasures of heaven. Loot the dragon's house.

Saying #39 "The Pharisees and the scholars have taken the keys of knowledge and have hidden them. They have not entered nor have they allowed those who want to enter to do so." This refers to the non disclosure of the manna as what it was and was actually for to God's children.

Saying #42 "be passersby" don't get stuck in the Dragon's world. Don't get off track and pursue the things of this world and make unnecessary things the goal of your life. Eyes on the prize.

Saying #49 " Congratulations to those who are alone (unattached) and chosen, for you will find the kingdom. For you have come from it, and you will return there again." The journey of experience through the dragon's world of death, from the kingdom of heaven and back to it again.

Saying #56 "Whoever has come to know the world, has discovered a carcass, (realized it is death) and whoever has discovered a carcass, of that person the world is not worthy." (to overcome the world is to overcome desire for its things- the world not worthy of them, the children of heaven)

Saying #62 "I disclose my mysteries to those who are worthy of my mysteries" The worthy will know.

Saying #66 "Show me the stone that the builders rejected, for that is the keystone" regarding the scribes, pharisees, sadducees, and high priests rejecting the use of manna in order to prepare the children of heaven for ascension.

Saying #92 "seek and you will find" you will not know what you have found if you are not seeking it.

Saying #102 "damn the Pharisees! They are like a dog sleeping in the cattle manger: the dog neither eats nor lets the cattle eat". Regarding their rejection of the use of the manna, and the hiding of the knowledge of what it is for.

Saying #108 "Whoever drinks from my mouth will become like me; I myself will become that person, and the hidden things will be revealed to him" Understanding Jesus, consuming the manna, realizing Christ in yourself, and achieving "true sight".

Saying #110 "let one who has found the world, and has become wealthy (with knowledge of truth), renounce the world." Surrender death.

The mormon plan of salvation is another way of describing the truth of the journey through the dragon's world. It states that we all have a premortal existence, but are sent down into the mortal world (in what is called the fall, or the first death) to live a lifetime (gathering experience), after which we go to a "world between worlds" called a "spirit world" where we are judged as a way of determining which world we go to after this world (after the dragons world), which they call the three kingdoms, Celestial, Terrestrial, and Telestial. With the Celestial kingdom being the kingdom of eternal life. ("I will give each one placement according to their works") Where those who exist, exist in God's presence. In the terrestrial kingdom dwell people who did not understand Jesus and believe in his "gospel" (understand him and follow his guidance) but were still honorable people who were generally kind and good people. In the telestial kingdom dwell those who continue to be guided by selfish desires, the untrustworthy who prey upon others.

If you believe in reincarnation, then reincarnation would happen within the dragons world. I see reincarnation as an aspect of a loving God who doesn't really want to destroy his children, but will allow them to suffer at the hands of the cruel treatment of the dragon's minions as long as they choose to, their eternal energy travelling through endless temporal lifetimes. Being born, struggling through the journey, and experiencing death, and losing their loved ones over and over again. The journey out, away from God, in the proving ground, they choose to stay on as long as they choose to not overcome selfishness. He created manna as a gift and a means to help them overcome it.

This is the story of the body I AM in. At the age of 24 I experienced a motorcycle crash. It ruptured my bodies intestines. During the surgery, I woke up outside my body and the dragon's world. In the world between worlds or "spirit world". A voice spoke inside me that said, "If you let go now, you will have failed to prove yourself", at which moment I replied, "then I'm not done yet, there is still something I need to do". As soon as I came to that "I'm not done yet" conclusion, the hospital room where I could see my body lying on the bed appeared before me as if it were an image on tv. The image got closer and closer and then suddenly, I was back in my body, in the hospital room. My body's stomach was stapled together from the surgery and I began to cry, because I knew that living a normal life, as a normal human, just working, trying to earn money, and being with friends, like so many do, had left me unfulfilled. I had lived a normal life and experienced death and heard that I was found unworthy. It was a beautiful tragedy that I had witnessed, realizing the judgment and sorting into the next worlds was real, and I had not passed. I knew that I had an opportunity to share my experience with the world, and will not fail. I had died, but did not die, and now I know the truth. The truth which I have been sent back into the dragon's world with, and an opportunity to share with you.

Leonardo da Vinci said many things, regarding works of art, that they are finished when they are abandoned, and one can have no greater mastery than that which is self mastery.

There have been many prophets throughout time trying to help those who just don't quite get it, to get it. Sadly, they will only get it if and when they choose to.

"To be or not to be" is the opening phrase of a theatrical play named "Hamlet" by William Shakespeare, in which the prince bemoans the pain, struggle, and fairness of "life".

Jesus said, saying #19 "Congratulations to those who come into being, before coming into being, of you this world is not worthy". Congratulations to those who become the children of God they truly are before it is time to leave the world of the dragon, they will be those God knew.

Human life is the opportunity to know one's self and understand God's plan, or not, is your choice. It is not easy, but those who choose to get it, do.

www.ingramcontent.com/pod-product-compliance
Lightning Source LLC
Chambersburg PA
CBHW080416170426
43194CB00015B/2829